The River I Know You By

The River I Know You By

Stephen Knauth

FOUR WAY BOOKS
Marshfield

 Please direct all inquiries to:

Four Way Books
PO Box 607
Marshfield, MA 02050

Library of Congress Catalogue Card Number : 98-72332

ISBN 1-884800-16-5

Cover art: CB Follett

Cover and text design: The Creative Team

Four Way Books is a division of Friends of Writers, Inc., a Vermont-based not-for-profit organization. Publication of this book was made possible by generous support from individual donors.

Acknowledgments

The Arts Journal: "The Lure"

AWP Newsletter: "I Thought Trees Were Separate Objects"

Blue Pitcher: "Hermitage"

Green Mountains Review: "Doing the Dishes," "Time Lapse"

Greensboro Review: "Butterfly Mind," "Patience"

Mississippi Review: "Nightfall"

The North American Review: "Wisteria"

The Pacific Review: "Fruit Trees"

Prairie Schooner: "White Ash (Garland of Purple Finch),"
"Horse," "Saturn Over Pisgah"

Southern Poetry Review:
"Early Autumn Evening, Little Pigeon River"

The Virginia Quarterly Review:
"On That Faint Hum I Hear In the Mountains at Night,"
"The Four Corners"

Thanks to the National Endowment for the Arts and to the North Carolina Arts Council for writing fellowships which assisted in the completion of this collection.

for my family

CONTENTS

I

Wisteria / 3

Hermitage / 4

Eta Carina / 5

Doing the Dishes / 6

Horse / 7

The Four Corners / 8

Blue Angel / 9

White Ash (Garland of Purple Finch) / 10

Grandfather with Wolves / 11

Geological Survey Map, Black Brothers, North Carolina, 1947 / 12

Truelight Church Road / 13

Night Tour / 14

Davidson River, Waking After Midnight / 15

God's Eye / 16

Watching My Father in the Yard at Dusk / 17

II

Monongahela / 21

Early Autumn Evening, Little Pigeon River / 23

Maybe Love / 25

I Thought Trees Were Separate Objects / 26

Testimony / 27

Nightfall / 28

III

Methuselah / 35
Delta Violet / 36
Gorget / 37
Pisgah Fragment / 38
Fruit Trees / 39
Patience / 40
Time Lapse / 41
Elizabeth / 43
The Lure / 44
Saturn Over Pisgah / 46
I Keep Driving / 47
Zinnias / 48
The Crossing / 49
Arctic / 50
Butterfly Mind / 52
Curtains, Sullivan's Island / 53
Edisto / 54
Red Giant, White Dwarf / 55
Still Life, Little Pisgah Mountain / 56
On That Faint Hum I Hear in the Mountains at Night / 57

IV

My Little Town / 61
The River I Know You By / 62

I

Wisteria

Over time wisteria wraps itself around the heart
and tightens. It twines and inquires, *When?*
The heavy sweet lavender-blue combs seem dream-like,
a bygone hue that speaks of regret and retired hope.
They seem to ask, *Was it so?*
Mother and father, the bare necessities—see them
grow shaggy as they bow toward Earth's rooms.
See them returning with their bushels full,
pulling them down. You knew, but kept your knowing
locked in a silver box at the back of the drawer,
a placeholder for lost faces, and the fact.
Gone, those who taught you to tell time are gone.
Now the clock face darkens, hands outstretched for payment.
Now who remembers your special name?
When at last you reach for the box,
the clasps are jammed. It takes a sharp blow
for you to remember, to see them once again,
as crisp as the day she died, as cruel,
delicate petals of asking blue.

Hermitage

High in the chipped hills
north of Spruce Pine
my cabin glows like a grounded star.

One cot, one table, two chairs.
The door stands open
without asking, *Won't you come in?*

The dead seem right here tonight,
huddled close like pigeons
in a cold steeple,

peaches in a jar.
Maybe they need one another
more than the living do?

All evening
breezes thread the rusty screens.
How quiet this place is,

clock on the mantle
stopped by time, glass wind chimes
shattered on the ground,

red threads fluttering from the eaves.
So quiet, miles from town.
All alone, alive

and gentled by my guests.

Eta Carina

Eta Carina, I dreamed of you again
last night, your fathomless blossoms
erupting along the black veins of Orion's arm.
Your sigh, captured by sleep's instruments,
spoke. I dreamed I understood you,
your longing. From your pictures I believe
you have known desire and suffering,
that perhaps your plumage maps the realms
of their interdependence, their wild marriage.
Older than mankind yet still an infant
in your world, what do you wish to be?
From my pebble-in-the-ocean I invite you:
pollinate my dreams with the powder of young stars,
with the blue light of your womb help me see.
Eta Carina, I don't recall what you whispered
last night. Only that when I awoke
the moon was low in the west,
and I was standing with the foxgloves by the gate.

Doing the Dishes

Shiver of light along the kitchen sill,
blade that breaks open the painted egg
inside me, blown and stenciled by time.
Never mind the stiffening layers of grief
that accumulate like newsprint in the shed.
Forget those-liquor-bottle-against-the-house
cries-in-the-night; childhood swallows them
like dark chocolate. Absolute indifference
is what the blade stuck me with, the whole's
ultimate apathy toward its parts—even the
message itself wavers uncertainly along the sash,
by-product of the light's daily death throes,
with a windy foreground of willow, like cilia,
to help move things along—*Next!* My hopes
and dreams scrolling into view, then yours.
Greek myth says, To gaze upon even the least
particle of God's finery would destroy us,
such is his glory. Is that it? That such power,
a single thread of whose garment cuts flesh,
cuts reason, lies fully outside the mind, giving
the appearance of nothing, of indifference?
The light dances in the corner. On, off.
Yes, no. The word I want is in between.

Horse

He circles me tonight,
Galactic Dark Horse,
whose fetlocks and withers

fill the black unbearable chasms
between stars, the very beast
Jesus saw that night

when he looked up to find
his way. The same creature
each earthly spirit rides homeward.

Dark brother, if we could see your body
would your purpose be clear? We want
to know, we don't want to know.

Your neighbors, bright nebulae,
boil with new stars
while you brood, out of sight, restless.

Tonight you canter across the summer sky
as we bend over papers
and books, over lovers and loved ones,

grooming the unknowable.

The Four Corners

My great uncles were twins,
two sets of them, born in the coalfields
of Alsace-Lorraine, where twins

make sense: one for the shovel,
one for the pick. Can't you
see them, seated across the lunchroom table,

dark hands rising and falling in unison?
The Four Corners, the other men
would whisper, and stand away.

See the great uncles nod in passing and descend!
See them as they would have been
but for the sorry facts. But for their tiny

skeletons, shining in the earth.

Blue Angel

Though it may not protect me
the Blue Angel Hosta does
instruct me. It says rise

up from the ground but
not too fast. Sway when
the wind whispers *sway.*

Give to the leaf what you
give to the bloom. Stay put.
Remember, the Blue Angel reminds me,

your beauty is made of rainwater and dirt.

White Ash (Garland of Purple Finch)

This afternoon I received a message
composed of several dozen purple finch—
the ones whose heads appear to have been dipped

in blood—flashing loudly along a battered limb
of white ash, squawking and picking at the down-hanging
clusters of narrow-winged keys,

their soft round bellies protruding
like cold fruit from the tree. Noisy garland
inscribed like a message overhead, or a placeholder

for a message, looking-glass of the heart.
Bough whose novembral leaves bear the stain
of a lost son, of abandoned faith half-regained.

Whatever spoils within you blazes darkly here.
Shines in an acid bath, scoured and mellowed,
until it becomes a feature of the outer world,

grafting you to the earth. He who
completes a message he cannot comprehend
stands for hours at the foot of a half-dead ash,

sending forth shoots.

Grandfather with Wolves

He knew it all and then forgot.
Seeker, sought-after, shell.
He looks out his window for the first time.

The sky is blue all right.
The moon's corpse drops behind the hardware.
In his dream a baby slips

from the pier to the murky water below,
comes up snagged on a hundred lines.
In his dream the pines

are seaworthy, nailed to the ocean floor.
Clouds of coral sperm, rising,
look like snow on the boughs.

What was that world
he knew at night and forgot,
kept remembering and forgetting?

He looks out the window
and wonders if dreaming isn't one of the elements,
flywheel that keeps the blood returning.

Dark song that runs beneath all forms of life.
At night we drink with wolves.
Drink with owls and forget.

Never mind not knowing.
At the center of existence
a black spider sleeps,

one leg on the signal thread.

Geological Survey Map, Black Brothers, North Carolina, 1947

In the Black Brothers Quadrangle
a blue vireo belts out its tune.
See-me? Here-I-am. Up-here. See-me?
Far below, a man studies the map,
his finger slowly tracing
the shape of the song drifting down.
These hills, old fender-bender
between continents—*North America*
and Africa collide! What a noise
that bird makes. It dislikes being
looked down upon, held between
dirty hands. Dislikes the numbers
scrolling in the traveler's eye.
True north, magnetic north—men!
April, bits of spirit caught on the branch tips.
The man keeps climbing.
He must reach Winter Star Ridge by noon
to make Blue Sea Falls by dark.
The bird sings. The man struggles.
The map does not say why.

Truelight Church Road

Up on Truelight Church Road I found
an asterisk of blood on the ground.
That one and no others. I sat down,
looked up into the negative space
between elms and wondered, not so
much about death—though perhaps
a hawk had captured a rabbit here—
as about the mind's urge to build
a cage for each thing—I hereby
explain and conquer thee! exclaims
the brain, as if no object or event
on earth could be too great to pass
from one synapse to another. A child
will learn that her deepest breath
only seems to make the stars burn
brighter, that the magnificent sum
of all that we know is merely a tic
on the wrinkled countenance of all
that we don't. Teach her, too, that
ancient saying I want to believe
is true today: *The snow falls,*
each flake in its appropriate place.

Night Tour

This is Original Darkness. First Dew
soaking our pant legs to the knee.
Blind folk at the edge of a meadow,
miles from camp, no moon, Little Sister Mountain.
The deer we cannot see see us.
For a moment it's almost enough.
Then we break out the night-vision goggles
that some vet brought back from the Gulf
and left with the ranger back at camp,
having seen too much through its eerie lens.
We pass the glasses, exchanging
our blindness for a gray-green gloom
inhabited by delicate, glowing creatures.
One by one, the silence reveals its layers—
insect, reptile, mineral, astral—of sound.
Breath by breath, the meadow's rhythm
claims us, until we cannot say how or when.
We climb the mountain at night
to see something we thought we knew.
But the deer we insist on seeing
are no longer here. They've wandered away,
leaving their pale costumes for us to try.

Davidson River, Waking After Midnight

Tonight the pines make that kitten sound,
the wind releasing their true voice. As sleep
releases the dream. As time, the soul.
Where have they gone, the ones who made us?
Who carved and painted us?
We stayed awhile on the shelf, then climbed down.
Desired what was cut away, withheld.
Into the world we floated with our hearts exposed,
vowing all shall be new. Found the future
comes furnished with the past.
Ascended the seven mountains of sand.
Where have they gone, those we're bound to follow,
whose essence death extracts and refines
and uses to lure us to the edge of the woods?
The pines cry softly in the summer night,
calling for those who feel ready.

God's Eye

Recall there is the perfectly calm, bottomless
pool at the center of the raptor's eye
where each reflection is numbered and stored.
Remember, at the center of the rabbit's eye.
Every thought, every cry is held suspended there,
spent coins eternally drifting downward.
Tonight I stare into the God's Eye my daughter made
at the Native American festival. Bright yarn
wound around crossed popsicle sticks.
Alternating bands of light, looking.
She could not decide on the first color, pupil
of the eye. *Your heart knows,* the helper said softly.
The heart says black, the heart says green.
The heart says all life is a single cell
that the brain has blown apart for pleasure.
The hawk awakens. The hare crouches down.
Perfectly calm, even at the moment of capture.
Especially at the moment of capture.

Watching My Father in the Yard at Dusk

As the sun drops below the roofline
the great house-shadow awakens
and glides out across the lawn
toward the iron chair of his afternoons,
slowly devouring him from the ground up,
until only his head is visible in the light,
slipping under, he seems, drowning,
yet the slight tuck at the corner of his mouth,
yet the calm cobra milk of his eye,
as if he had pinched a small victory from time,
from circumstance, and now,
now he is returning to his country.

II

Monongahela

I felt the season turning today,
reflection of a white Impala in the pond,
the dreamy impermanence of it—didn't the elders say
that water is a membrane between worlds?
Say *Sep-tem-ber* is the sound of rain through the pines?
These carved models of dead Canadian geese,
placed here and there to discourage the real thing,
give sea gulls a place to stand. Rounding the shore,
a rope-line of preschoolers, day campers,
orange of their matching shirts caught by the water's lens,
dim procession of torches, *this way, this way, weary soul, come.*
Turning, if only the weather inside me, something
about the flight home last night. We took off near dusk,
and I remember looking down through choppy clouds—
great North American motherboard flickering on—
looking down and back, over my shoulder,
thinking that must be Pittsburgh, thinking green sparks
of the Monongahela struck my eye. I started to ask
the attendant, but let her pass. I let memory
pass, or bypass, logic. Let the pictures come
and go, voices deep indwelling. My father's face,
strobing on and off, driving through the Liberty Tubes at night,
piercing the mountain's black heart, no words, no
sweat, ribbons of "Turkish" tobacco smoke floating between us,
Steve and Eydie, creamy smooth, rejoining us as we crossed the river.
Childhood's lost and the found, rummage around and take what fits.
How many others, alone and strapped down, do the same?
Then I noticed my hand, high above the earth,
reaching for my book, how my skin had grown thin,
tissue paper thin, with faint brown spots, like the hands
of my mother's dad, who lay so quietly on the davenport
the only time I ever saw him, so still, cloudy slits

of his eyes showing me the future clearly.
When I turned and looked back the river was gone;
I put down my book and dozed.
Today, geese look down, see what remains of their kind
and land anyway. They pave the paths with their waste,
turn the water green, yet carry themselves with perfect grace
as they cross the water, leaving a gentle wake upon the heart.
Passing by, they deepen feelings too faint or too strong
to be spoken. Sometimes I think
my mother conveyed her deepest thoughts to us
by marking passages in books—an occasional star
in the margin, a swirling bracket—and then
loaning the books to us, or leaving one by the bedside.
Reading, we held our silent conversation. Time turns us
on its invisible lathe, cutting away what's not true,
what can't be kept. Is that what I sense, sitting here,
the Earth turning, already, too soon, as it must, without us?

Early Autumn Evening, Little Pigeon River

In heavy woods
an elm leaf makes
its way to the ground.

A bird creaks far off, then near.

The Little Pigeon arcs and swaggers
through last-minute searching stalks of light.
Beautiful, this spotlit rock,

this smoking triangle of water,
by turns falling helplessly away
into darkness. Who

wouldn't mind going
that way, fast and pretty,
an elegant dance step to the left?

Beautiful, the way the river proceeds
without us, proceeds and proceeds
under a funny grape sky.

The brainstem darkens.

Things darken
as the sound of the river rises
in the ears of a thirsty housebroken man.

As, in the shrinking distance,
in no wind at all,
another leaf

that wasn't ready
a moment ago,
goes.

Maybe Love

The young diver is pinned by the giant clam again,
his left leg crushed by the valves. Probably will drown again
and in death be contacted by the same blind *itako,*
though she will seem a stranger. The message
she carries to his loved ones will be cherished by them, as before.
In this way another layer of experience is deposited.
In this way the pearl grows round. And rounder still
by each rotation of night skaters at Cannonsburg Dam—
those that slip beneath the ice are quickly replaced—
round and round under the naked-eye planets,
under stars that are themselves mortal,
ignited and snuffed out like Monarchs.
Maybe love is the grease that makes it go.
Maybe death. The one who knows is far back in the forest,
deeper than the body can go. Way back
where the willow rejoins the water and the sky.
The one who keeps the necklace of names
and the six, sacred shrouds:
mother, father, sister, brother, daughter, son.

Note: In Japan, blind women, called *itakos*, are believed to possess the ability to communicate with the spirit world.

I Thought Trees Were Separate Objects

I thought trees were separate objects
until I saw them joined in the woods that day
by innumerable long and ghostly filaments of *stuff.*
I wondered then, do spiders fly?

I've since imagined them everywhere,
long loose stitches binding the world together,
each man sewn to his kin, to each blade of fescue
that bends down beneath him,
to his own incessant picture of the world
that dances like Isadora just out of reach.

Along the lines, death gives a mighty tug
but the connections hold, glistening downward
through cool mist that gushes from fresh-broken ground.
How far we would sink without tombstones to tread on!
Without the replenishing memory
and rememory of death.

Like marigolds begun in a dim pantry
and set out to harden in the gentle morning sun,
we toughen and reach out, into the future, into the past,
lugging our tangled rootballs along.

I thought trees were separate objects
until I stopped looking and saw them that day
down by the lake, indivisible, as darkness
passed over the county like an eyelid slowly closing.
Transfixed, as up from the grave
my death came ringing, like a team of strong horses,

the reins in my hand.

Testimony

By sepals and pistils we are summoned
to testify against almighty darkness,
to unfurl our hatred in the presence of daffodils.
Down the throats of lilies we pour our bile.
Their sheer indifference is what attracts us,
nectar of not judging. Pausing among them
seems to weaken time, make the past wait.
Here, waist-deep in cool flames, the widow
burnishes her pain. Here the child,
wrongly accused, curls toward sleep,
calls to dinner floating like birdsong above.
The pausing-place, where silence grows
and where forgiveness is held
inviolate.

Nightfall

In our little patch at nightfall
the doomed ones have their say.
They have their song, and die.

Come, memory, my bread,
silver grains melting at the mind's edge.
Childhood is a planet.

Its golden ruins, a star.

•

It's snowing hard in Allegheny County.
It is always snowing *then*. Brown ice
on the Monongahela. Three rivers,

two tunnels, one fate to elude.
Already the snow has buried the scout tent entirely.
Inside, a boy huddles, listening.

He hears the flakes' ghostly murmuring,
hears and obeys. Feels a dread
joy unfolding.

All night, memory says, the snow
continued. Memory says the boy
emerged from his cocoon,

his new body steaming in the yard.

•

Come, intensify the fallen light.
We know the core of the Earth
spins faster than its surface,

not unlike the human heart,
which seems to always arrive
before the rest of us. Not unlike

our ability to receive, after loss,
the smallest songs in the ivy, ones
we never knew were there,

signals from beyond the band.

•

Remember—I do—the backs of the necks
of the men in the Sunday congregation?
Prickly, puckered, bloated fruit.

Mute sermon I still recall, telling
what faith cannot forestall. I stared,
sang when my father gripped my kneecap.

Sang about the blessed child, and the blessed
day—a mighty fortress of bristling necks—
and when the Host came round, I ate, One.

At the door, heading for their cars,
I turned and saw their faces, saw the lamb
and the wolf entwined. I saw

and took my father's hand.

•

All of us here together,
fragile carbon-based forms of life,
gathered together in the evening breeze,

another millennium winding down,
pear tree, field cricket, middle-aged man
kindling memory, slowly opening

each of ten thousand silver cages.
Multitudinous cries of desire
rising and falling, steady hum

that keeps the planet turning.

•

Through the back door crack we could
see them, garish faces suspended
like bulbs in soil. *Iron City,*

Black Label, whose light suffices.
Through the smoldering crack
we saw, then scattered.

Fathers at the Green Lantern,
their faces different.
Floating, floating,

freed of their stems.

•

Strike a pack of matches for the poplars in the west.
For the smoke not the flame.
Winter not fall.

Ridge from which Pittsburgh
was a smudge and a glint
thirty raw miles away.

Snow, it was
snow that made us build God,
brick by brick, of words.

We had iron fathers
melted by gin,
work.

Even then the dim
light of a sickroom
leaked from their eyes.

That hill, Gilfillan's
farm, flush of our bodies
the only color for miles.

Crows
in their places,
each black atom carved by a patient hand.

The years, unspooling,
always snag
on those pale trees.

The war just over,
another coming on.
Clemente in right field.

Vernon Law on the mound.
Looks good, looks good,
Dad would say.

But my tongue had turned to ore.

•

Alone in the darkened yard
a grainy ray of moonlight breaks through the pear trees,
softly striking the knuckles of my left hand:

old chapped yellow hills.
From far away, from around the farthest bend,
my hand glows at the receiving end

of an ancient third-party transaction.
I open my palm and begin to read—
you already know.

I want to lie down and can't.
I sit, holding the moon by its fragile stem,
remembering clearly, as the pears dip and straighten,

the sound of my mother's voice calling from deep in the house.

III

Methuselah

It's time to take up the long narrow spatula—the kind used
to remove brownies from a pan—and harvest the golden corpses of summer,
hollow husks of Japanese beetles accumulating all summer on the sill.
Shovel them up, the season's done; start anew, the end draws near. By now
they weigh almost nothing, like the remains of the person you dreamed of becoming
under the smooth dome of childhood. Every summer evening they come,
mid-July through late August, a half dozen each night, their terrible engines
driving them toward the light, flipping on their backs, legs treading air, until...
I tried but could not keep them out. Spackled the panes, patched the screens,
which only seemed to encourage them, and verify my ineptitude. Daddy!
my daughter cries as a bronze monster attacks her study lamp.
I come with my single sheet of Kleenex, catch and release, like a fly fisherman
over the limit, catch and release—only to return that same night?
Once I thought to dab them with different colors of nail polish, just to see.
Once I thought to acquire a crow and let him rule the house by night.
Oh ignoble sill dwellers of September—horse flies, mosquitoes, and ladybugs too—
it's time to bring forth the heavy white mortar and pestle, the one that's good
for mashing cumin seeds into coarse black powder. Grinding the summer beetles!
Grinding them up for the tiny fish in the back yard fountain. One fish, really—
all that remains of the ten-for-a-dollar batch we bought last month
at Pet Palace. My son scatters the offering solemnly on the surface of the water—
bright and dark flecks, floating for a moment like ashes on the Ganges—
until the lone survivor ascends swiftly from the depths, confirming his name.

Delta Violet

Walking out over the old sea bed
to pick up a package of cigarettes,
out through the prevailing layer—
Wal-Mart, Best Buy, BlockBuster, Sam's—
present day mastodons who will miss?
Mr. Toursi, Pittsburgh middle school
gym teacher, tough as toenails, told me,
Son, you won't last long. I didn't,
we won't, so relax and let go, awake
to what's already headed our way.
By that I don't mean don't pay attention.
Christ keep me quiet in a world where,
on the landlady's tongue, *pansy* blossoms
into *Delta Violet, with Face.* Where death
comes back in a different cloak each time,
unique as the heart it seals in amber.
Toe the line, up to it but not on it!
Mike Toursi barked. The line
some of us had already crossed,
that others would never cross, caught
on youth's barbed gate. Those boys,
what would they give? Just to shave
their chins and walk out into the night!
Fretted bars of natural light unfurl
in the scrap of sky between the BP
and Rooms To Go. Just that tint,
reminding me that the garden thrives,
garden of nonrefundable love—spent,
spilt—wilderness only the heart can harrow.

Gorget

Gorget, the hummingbird's throat patch,
is my beacon on these dreary days.
Its iridescence, its sound. *Gorget.*
A small device is required to halt time,
to roll back the heart's high mileage,
zero out those big plans and nagging doubts.
A bird will do. A low gust in saw
palmetto. Instant of pure attention,
as when the elder peels away the boy's
foreskin, and the past disappears:
Anno Domini. As when Shiva's dwarf
curls up at your feet, bloated with desire.
Dreary days, little comets lighting the eaves.
I'm standing, I'm turning in the yard,
whose cedars scour the sky.

Pisgah Fragment

Black marble, white marble,
surface of the river at night.
Our camp on the bank, Lilliputian.
Facing the fire, where the gold
bars of time's passage are forged.
Trying not to think, and thinking
of something someone said
on the radio last night:
Slow the tempo
to enlarge the beat.
Long braids of light and dark
carry the mountain downward.
The fire's red mouth
speaks. How many
years do I have left to listen?

Fruit Trees

Domestic trees
outside my window
look ominous and wild
when half past seven
enamels their branches.
It's then that the difference
between things fails, words
fail, *asterisk* and *asteroid*
sputter and misfire across
the darkening hemispheres
of the mind. Narrative fails
though the hand keeps
crawling over the page,
encircling the wreckage.
Eight, nine, ten o'clock...
As another day escapes,
the trees succeed in trapping
time between their branches.
There, in the stillness
surrounding each blossom, it
gathers and steeps, ripening
until all the hours of summer
are suddenly unleashed
upon the wordsick
cherry-seeking
tongue.

Patience

Through the grimy window of the No. 19 bus
I saw her, standing in front of Mel's Tax Haven,
long ash of her face perfectly balanced,
lips pursed, refusing to kiss misfortune,
one eye pasted shut, the other, green solitaire
refracting my gaze. By that first glimpse
I knew her message could not reach me all at once,
that her expression was a slow-motion explosion
of meaning, like the blue whale's song, *infrasonic,*
its notes so low, so long, the human ear can't
detect it, but if recorded and speeded up
thirty times normal, it sounds like a mourning dove
or a hungry owl. Lovely, she is, in the way
of the other world. Other-lovely in her red parka,
hood zipped tight, holding the arrangement in place.
Each morning, I'm waiting here. *Patience,*
I call her. Some songs take a lifetime to sing.

Time Lapse

Now starlings come
and the thicket turns to sugar.
Colors of the atlas deepen
in the imperious after-dinner light.
By the stove, by the window,
the year comes round, unfaltering.
We live in the past imperfect,
gone but not dismissed.
Would you, if you could, forget?
Sparks of the welder's torch,
would you care to put them back?
Fifty thousand starlings
chatter in the scrub oaks.
This is the moment we live for!
My son and I rush into the yard,
pause, then clap our hands sharply—
oh vast familiar millisecond of silence
followed by that unutterably magnificent
nearly sexual upsurge of wings!
For the longest time, it seems,
we watch them, wave after wave,
darkening the sky like Judgment,
departing, yet somehow remaining,
five-hundred-mile-bolt-of-dark-cloth,
eclipsing time, watching for so long
that my son seemingly grows to manhood,
while I grow weak, weaker, and then
pass entirely away—why not?—the birds
taking me, me looking back at him,

my boy—man!—down there in the yard,
his right hand shading his eyes, the left
in a fist, slashing the air, as if to say,
Go, Dad! All right, Dad! Beautiful!

Elizabeth

Wicked evening, rainy cold,
rocking my daughter
back and forth in time,
her birth to my death,
All the Pretty Horses
taking us there.

The Lure

Venus is in the lindens tonight.
It's nice to see some
land up there.

To the west,
a few good stars,
enough to remind us

how grand our manners,
how bright our coins.
The kind of evening—

warm, chin-lifting breezes—
when a lawn chair on the deck
is an aerie

on a crag,
when the whole steaming world
lay spread before us like dinner on the ground.

God must have known from the start
we'd discover forbidden routes,
follow them inward

to the spot where our names
have been bitten
into stone,

to that shady grove
behind the eyes, dim triangle
between the projector and the floor.

He knew,
built these stars
to lure us back,

gave us language
as a net to trap them,
and distributed, here and there,

the incurable belief that we conceivably could.

Saturn Over Pisgah

Can you hear them tonight,
big sisters hissing in the void?
Can you, in your dreams, while
I explore the mysterious delta
at the bend of your left knee?
I know nothing but your breathing
here on Pisgah's floor,
our fire progressing to embers.
Asleep, I can ask you now,
Doesn't some part of us go on?
Memory, regret, anger, pride—
what wheels will they turn?
Your mercy, what loom?
Last night, during the lunar eclipse,
we saw Saturn through a borrowed scope,
saw the toy beast for the first time.
Saw Jupiter, too, tiny with its tiny moons
lined up in a straight corner shot.
Forty-five years it took me to focus,
to feel Saturn alive inside me,
cardboard rings transformed to golden ice,
to stroke Jupiter's stormy face,
whirling without us for billions of years.
Asleep, I can ask you, How?
Sometime between midnight and dawn,
a light plane passes overhead,
coals of a hundred campfires visible below.
The plane banks slowly to the west.
What will our passion become?

I Keep Driving

Driving the old state roads again today—
washing my eyes with a cool green cloth.
Tail feathers of the jay tempered to pierce the heart.
Sweet steaming clods of earth upturned, faces
where tears have yet to run. Radio says
Kashmiris continue to fight over a true hair
from the beard of the prophet Muhammad. Says clouds
then clear. Driving west against the earth's spin,
into the wind, into the past. The old way
looks almost new today. New cows, new pond,
new man-with-boy coming down the road, rifle in his hand.
Our glances meet; his head cocks back.
I just keep driving, as if I were free.

Zinnias

Face down in dirt the old zinnias
wait for nothingness to ravish them, for the blind
and tender stroking-away. After dinner,
when shade of the holly is drawn across the stoop,
the names of the dead may be spoken again.
Spoken in that glass voice, glass cable under the sea.
Snow your hand is white as, melting on my wrist—speak.
Say it. Out in the fields where it can season and burn slow,
burn to embers, cold gems which cannot be extinguished.
Say the names, the ones whispered in hospital rooms,
say how he wept for life while combing his hair,
say how she bared her teeth like a wolf
on the last blurry downbeat of the heart. Say your pain
out loud on the front steps in the plush upholstered light.
Then bow, like the flowers, and wait.

The Crossing

Crossing the narrows you sense a royal light,
submerged, just beneath grief's surface,
descending. An island of rest to make for,
but like the moon along the river road
it keeps slipping away. Crossing the narrows
the depths stoke the heart with a silver note,
Still. Embery, not there, there—remember?
When the trip to town became a difficult voyage.
When your tongue ached from rowing words.
Friends and neighbors approach, the surface
reflecting their true faces. But what lasts?
Wise ones say the sea may enter the dew drop.
Perhaps, but the feeling goes. Even if it's
inside you, or you it, the heart wanes,
leaving its gentle liability.

Arctic

Like the rare blue bear
we cross the ice alone.
A great hunger warms us.

A hunger to know less.
To not know how love
grinds to glacial flour.

To not know our own
father's heart, crouch
in its lair and touch

the scraps of its meal.
We cross alone and see
fit to keep our world

away. Everything
just as the last ice left it,
emotional moraine

we know the edges of,
know the lonely burn of.
Snows you won't see

until you've joined us.
Until one evening
you find in the mirror

that quiet crevasse
through which your soul
can gently descend, has

been descending all along.
Ah, what lovely drifts we
we would have made had

ground been there to hold us.

Butterfly Mind

Little Wood Satyr
clinging to a wet stone
speaks in a dim, wound-around voice.
In bright sun, a song of darkness?
Of captivity, in the hour of freedom?
No, its umber wings open, close,
saying only, *I am drinking,*
I am drinking,
here in the fragile confection of now.

Curtains, Sullivan's Island

All night they keep coming,
quilted bars of the sea unceasing,
uncovering the heart's treasure, its deepest wrecks.
Tucked among the dunes, frail plank house
from whose open window, every few seconds,
pale curtains flutter into view, in time to the breathing
of the lovers within, perhaps, unfurling over the palms,
hesitating an instant, then falling, lightly dipping
the dark sea water, white fire on black fire, in and out,
while a man watching from a rental across the road
writes, *Which is better, leaving the world*
or returning to it? He likes to record his thoughts
before bed, then let the condensation of his drinking glass
make of them a lovely and meaningless lagoon.
Three nights a week he dreams of going under—
the others are merely nightmares.
He moves from town to town, dream to dream,
watching, dissolving, one grain at a time,
the past, its high cliffs, the future, its high cliffs.
Dissolving the ruined wharves and spires of the South,
the golden calf of a woman's leg. He knows
how night undoes the day, how they travel entwined,
braiding the sun's hair while he sleeps, his desires
floating quietly on the bedside table. In the morning,
he tapes the dried page—bleary sunset of purples
and blues—to the mirror and goes out.
Just now, he's standing perfectly still in the road,
staring without expression at the little dune-house
where last winter's plastic window sheeting
flaps crudely from a rusted nail.

Edisto

Superior cloudwork to the east.
Light rain, sun, hard rain, mist.
Two gods appear on the beach
contending over the corpse of a blue crab.
Moon-driven waves driven nowhere.
We spread the blanket, setting our place at the banquet.
Chaos, outer garment of divinity,
embraces our quaint squalor.
Along the tide, luminous shell fragments
foretell the rapture of the tomb, the dreamy razor cuts
of the days between death and death's acceptance,
between loss and surrender. There,
the rundown *whys* of our kind echo unheard.
But spread the feast of crackers and juice—what matters more?
On shaky toes, little sister interprets the sea,
then points to the clouds and calls them by name:
serious, cumulonimbulo. At seven thirty
the sun comes down in a bloody, punctual mess.
We set out candles and wait for The Crab.
We lean back in our rusty chairs, and belong.

Red Giant, White Dwarf

At Price Lake the fire's slow deliquescence
restores the lie that we'll be saved
when the earthly world goes up in flames.
So this is immortality, slouched in lawn chairs,
sipping cherry cola braced with *Cutty Sark*,
our faces just beginning to cool? And it does us
good, for now, to believe we'll finally reign,
our towering sins burned to the ground.
Like the sailmaker's palm we need some device
to protect our hearts from oblivion's needle.
A mental contraption to keep hope warm
even as we rake the world's coals and straggle to bed.
In the tent my son wakes up and wants to know.
At the science museum in town today, he heard
how the sun will grow, in five billion years,
into a red giant that will swallow the Earth
and then slowly shrink to a white dwarf.
He wants to know, Who will be left
to slice open the dwarf and pull the Earth out?
Who will stuff his belly with rocks, sew it up,
and push him down the well? Before I can tell him
a lie, or some moldy version of the truth,
he's asleep again. I lay back
and try to stop thinking, stop explaining.
Then I hear my savior, in the cattails,
in the rosebay, scraping his long dark legs.

Still Life, Little Pisgah Mountain

The fire is ripe now,
falling softly through the boughs
of consciousness.

Open on one side,
trembling
geode part of me wishes to enter,

to touch its heart wall
and know, to feel the burn
on the road to weightlessness.

There's an eye blue
in the flames—but whose?
Or it's the blue of runway lights

seen through a rainy cabin window
on the outskirts of which
lost and crumbling city of the East?

Something pulls at the lake.
Sleep, you mutter.
Old logs glowing like trinkets.

Sleep, whose planets are banked and waiting.

On That Faint Hum I Hear in the Mountains at Night

In your breast there's a black box
that tells what happened.
How you lost altitude or gained faith.
Where you started, wound up, went wrong.
What you really believed
and how your heart melted when you knew.
Who you loved, and how long, which names
detonated softly in your mind at the end.
The little box remembers
and shall be recovered,
shall be opened, shall be heard,
its contents distilled to a single note
and entered, patiently, in the score.

IV

My Little Town

Thoughts of you strafe my mind tonight,
materializing out of nowhere, fast and low,
taking out the white steeples and rose arbors
of the little town I built—lovingly, by hand—
to pretend that it's all okay. No matter where I hide
you seem to find me, and maybe I want that, maybe
after making sure everything is calm and well-kept.
I want to be driven screaming through the rustic square,
chess tables and potted chrysanthemums crashing,
dogs yelping, jerking their napping owners from their chairs.
Called by the merry executioner forward into the past—
Ah, now your heart must die so that cherry petals may begin to fall.

The River I Know You By

The world of dew
is the world of dew.
And yet, and yet—
—Issa

1

Lying in bed, half-remembering
how they stood in your room's doorway—
physician, metaphysician, priest—
their gowns in flames.
Your deep gaze was the river that saved them,
baptizing their failure.

2

It's coming clear now, there in the second tier of sight.
A small circle of elders, old women and men
facing one another in the forgotten way, their arms
reaching toward the circle's glimmering center,
toward something I can't quite see. Yet I know,
I know. They don't or can't speak. Contrails of white hair
that never stop growing. Entranced, they lean forward, faceless,
into a common shadow, as if joined in sacred ritual—
or simply warming their hands.

3

We received your letter last night,
cold pane of moonlight in the slot.

4

From the kitchen window, six views of the moon.
Six views of our quiet, cratered fate. If words
could travel like light across the spheres
and arrive intact, between whisper dishes of parent and child,
what would you say? What one word?
The past, its iron trees. I plow through dark
like a star-nosed mole, feeling my way through earth,
roots. I can't see you with my eyes.
Digging, to get closer. Digging, if only to impress
faint hope upon the heart.
Weary from its journey, moonlight passes
through poplars, through panes,
and comes to rest on the wall above the stove.
There, with blackened potholders, it rests.
Blank squares of light, calendar of what shall not be.

5

More than the bull I fear
the picador who lances the neck muscles of the bull,
to keep its head down for the charge. More than God,
the man who carves God's law. Some people
pray to stop remembering. Some bow so deep
they break in two. These faint soundings, at night,
as we lie within lunar currents, what
message is traveling toward us and from where?
What unbroken rose of unknowing? At dawn,
I wake up, afraid. Then I hear your voice,
sound of apples melting back into the ground.

6

Step into the shadow, then the umbra,
blackest part of shadow. And deeper still,
into the warren where the ruined mother lives.
She's waiting for you there, her arms shaped
round an emptiness. When she speaks she sounds
like a rake pulled through broken glass.
But listen to her, letting her words
flow in black transfusion between you,
draining the wound. Go, she is waiting.
Her body is swollen with grief.
She needs you. She reaches out and makes that sound.
She wants to fill you with knowing until you go down.

7

Returning to the river, day after day,
like a mistle thrush to the mistletoe.
Waiting for your paper boat to sail by.
Waiting for the leaves to get back on the trees.
        Leave your messages by the willow's root,
there to be claimed by the tide. Regrets
and questions. Place them here.

8

Keep it closed, creel of those days,
the hooks, the torn mouths, the stink.
The green surface of the pond instead,
with its greener reflections of willow and rue,
the face of the deep before we were swallowed.
Can we remember the solid feel of that world,
of the bottom beneath our feet? Our opinions
polished and arranged on the shelf, thus.
Our desires, our demands, our dominion.
Before the view was cinched and crumpled—can we?
Did we shed that life in order to grow?
Would we shrink, if we could, and crawl back in
to look out on that safe and ordered scene again?
You've seen those burned-out country places, what
remains—chimney, oil tank, bulbs that keep coming back
year after year along the edges of the old foundation.
Until one day in the woods you stumble
across a ragged right angle of iris, palest blue, smaller now,
more leaf than bloom, deeply rooted, ownerless, and wild.

9

The trail breaks down beyond the blue datura,
dissolving into the pale throat of the pond.
Become passers-by, the gospel says.
Hold lightly to what does and does not happen.
Who owns the breeze that blows the kudzu silver?
Who threads the comet's tail?
The best gifts are shaded with loss.
By the time its *kyrie* reaches me
the bird is out of sight.

10

Moonlight, demilune, dark.
When dream countermands
reality. When time is resting.
The factory glows in the distance.
The star factory, Tarantula Nebula.
Young blue stars born without notice—
your covers slip to the floor.
Cedars whorled like great cocoons
open. They open and show what's next.
Others are present at the watering place,
drinking our reason. Not the dead.
Not the enemy. All the same now.
All the same in such light.

11

Did I stand too long, staring up at the trees,
watching the colors deepen as the shadows
slid slowly away to the east? How they
bound me, the poplars and pines together,
the leaves and needles intermarried by fate,
alternating gold and green, the family
pattern, *Joy and Sorrow*, handed down.
Did I get too close to that world? To the
stained threshold of consciousness, oft-
crossed, polished with confusion and regret.
Did I stray too far from my kind? When I
turned to leave I found a silver strand—
as if plucked from Methuselah's head—
glimmering between a leaf stem
and the sleeve of my winter coat.

12

The bayonet through your heart is just
the first ray of your new life,
I want to tell a friend in pain. To say,
you will be remade, of glass and silver parts
with a little hammer that trips
when the crepe myrtle flames in the dooryard of August,
when the nightjar calls at the close of the day.
The hooks being pulled through your body
will grow dull and familiar. I touch
her shoulder and do not say, one day
you may even wish to sharpen them.

13

Summer's plush ruins, cattle cooling down.
The moon is a miner's light ascending its ancient shaft,
crossing the county at midnight, house by house,
dreamer by dreamer, bathing known
in unknown, melting the day's pain.
Restless, she takes her place by the window.
Looking into her face I feel the heavens lock,
clang shut over a land of regret and watery sleep.
Wondering if she hears me, I tell her about the wing
I found on the road today, wing of a butterfly,
of a Purple Hairstreak, how I held it to the falling
light and saw the very cell structure of sorrow.
That's us, caught in the black border that encircles the eyespot,
stranded, struggling, between the heat of its orange interior
and green rectangles of surrounding light.
How I watched the wing's delicate sundown, then placed it
gently—absurdly!—on the grass, as if its owner might flutter by
on one wing to claim it. I tell her this,
and in telling, cross over.

14

Now it's beginning to rain or else
a car is turning down the gravel road.
The grizzly male is solitary but …
tv's last words before bed.
A cloud passes the moon,
igniting the past, disturbing the nested years.
In spider-light a question crawls,
close by, through leaves, unasked, alive.
Pass by, pass by, the burnt heart says.
Do not ask and do not answer.
To bed, to my ragged listening post,
where I detect the whine of a light plane
lost in fog over Warrior Mountain
or else it's a child's cry, faintly,
faintly, through the membrane.

15

That lone cloud-stroke in the west,
so pale and diffuse it resists being.
Not cloud, not sky. As I watch it
pass between concepts, I realize
I shall not brush your hair again.

16

These are the vigil days, from Thanksgiving to Christmas,
the last days, during which we labored to bring forth death.
When the morphine suppositories glowed
like royal larvae in the butter dish of the refrigerator.
Underwater days, when we swam from room to room,
our cries trapped in bubbles of gas. Silent, unmentionable days.
When it was over, our relief, the shame of our relief.
Months later, our freefall surprised us—hadn't we
already touched down? We fell through the sea and the sea floor
to the center of the earth where the iron shrouds of grief are forged.
Fell *through* love, down the cinder cone of unanswered prayers,
through the mantle to the core, there to be recast into gargoyles, bells.
Through sorrow's filter the world is sharper, softer.
Passing laughter, its jagged edge, rakes open the wound.
Needles of the shortleaf pine, cresting in the breeze, sew it closed.
The truth it took years to confess: we were never so alive as then.
Never so human, never so free to follow the heart's command.
Never so unleashed, so feral, so stripped down, so *used*.
The vigil days come round again, become a vigil of remembering.
But not in words, not now, no words. More like notes
to a familiar song we hum inaudibly to ourselves.
The silence itself recalls what's missing, what's done.
So we sit, in the very room, almost at peace, candle on the sill,
and speak not of our fine young guest.

Stephen Knauth is the author of four previous collections of poetry, including *Twenty Shadows* (Four Way Books). He has published in many national journals, and has twice received creative writing fellowships from the National Endowment for the Arts. He has also been awarded fellowships from the North Carolina Arts Council. A native of Hales Corners, Wisconsin, he grew up in the Pittsburgh area and graduated from Ohio University. He currently lives with his family in Charlotte, where he works as a writer.